Conversations with Mr. Hooker
Volume 9

Poems and Songs of the Columbia Gorge revised

Don Hooker

Welcome to this the newest volume of poems and songs by Mr. Hooker in the Conversations with Mr. Hooker series. These are an accumulation of some previously published works from earlier volumes as well as new and unpublished pieces.

Mom and two sisters moved here to the Gorge in the 1980s. That's over thirty years of visiting the Gorge to see family over the years. A lot of changes here as this area worked to overcome a regional depression that lasted decades. Now thanks to local industries and agriculture, the tourist industry and some tech companies, the area is experiencing some pretty healthy growth. Local politicians and authorities are pretty much asshats but other than that the locals are good people. Hopefully this next election will get us some fresh and progressive people to clean things up. There are a lot of creative types here in the Gorge, seems hard to talk to a local person who is not an artist in some form or another. It is here in the Gorge that I found my creative bone and came to the point of saying that I too am an artist. Any good or not you can decide for yourself.

The Gorge itself is, I believe is one of Gods finest works. The beauty and grandeur are extraordinary. Here in the west Gorge we are between two powerful mountains, Mount Hood to the south and Mount Adams to the north. With Columbia River running down the middle. Not to mention the dozens of other rivers and streams flowing into the Columbia.

I hope you enjoy this book, all of works are mine, are based on my experiences and or imagination. If you have the chance to visit the Gorge please keep Hood River and White Salmon on you list of places to visit. Thank you and God bless.

Riding the river tonight

Come on down to the Gorge tonight
Come on down in the pale moon light
Come on down to the river bank
Drop you board in the water tonight
Feel the water wash you clean
Let the wind set you free
Come on down to the Gorge tonight
Ride the river in the pale moon light

Careful

It's a slippery slop
When you walk to the
Tarwater
In the snow
If you're not careful
You will take a fall
Right on your butt
But going down is ok
To slide to the front door
For a beer and Jager shot
But going up…

When the sun first breaks

When the sun first breaks
Across the hills in the morn
It shines its red across the land
And onto the river
Once in the river the red is carried along
Soon it looks like the river is aflame
With a fire in the water
But just as fast as it came
The red is gone from the land
And gone from the water
But watch tonight
Far to the west and out of sight
You will see the red creep in
On the side of the mount
And down the hill
Into the water and just for while
You see the river red
With the flames of the sunset
Soon to lose out to the darkness
Lose out to the night
But in the morn
When the sun first breaks

Small town love and lust
Shhhhhh let's not talk
About this in the open
Let's not talk about this
Too loud
No one to hear us
But let's be discreet
And not talk in the street
Let's step into here or
Over there
I feel better in a confined space
For this is not something
I wish to face
But certainly not here
This is a small town
Someone will
know something
Is a miss
But only you and I know
That this is anything
At all
It may be nothing
But a night of lust
Or could it be that we trust
Our feelings of each other
Neither here or there
For the time being
Let's just sit and enjoy
Before anyone knows

The river flows
Rev 07/2018

Down by the river
The water flows along
Swift and steady as she goes
Always on the move
Sometimes she is high
On the bank
And others she is low
On the bank
But always she flows
Right past the bank
And so we sit and watch
Or we move along with it
Or maybe we just drive on by
And hardly glance at it
The river gives no mind
The water flows along
Swift and steady she goes
She cares not where you are going

Foothills

Scanning the horizon
The hills
I have never lived
Close to the foot hills before
See the snow atop in the winter
The underbrush and grasses
Green in the spring
Brown in the summer
Fires in the late summer
And early fall
How the clouds hover
On the top of the hills
Before spilling over
Into the Gorge
Always drama in the hills
All you have to do is notice

Spring in the Gorge

Its spring in the Gorge
And it's snowing
It's snowing
Spring in the Gorge
Irises blooming
Irises blooming in the snow
As it's snowing it's snowing
Spring in the Gorge

Mount Hood
Rev 07/2014

I watch the country side
Roll by
The orchards
The farm land
The small towns
The mountain getting closer
Can't see it today
Due to the clouds
But I can feel it
When one stands between the
Mountain and the river
The power of the river so close
Is overwhelming
Though you still feel the mountain
But as you travel up the hills
To the base of Mount Hood
You can feel the chill in the air
Your breath a little harder
You feel heavy on the ground
The power of such a renegade mountain
Known for its sudden storms
How many dead
Never recovered from the Hood
One slip and you are falling
To a place no one has ever
Seen the bottom of
Both the river and the mountain

Are dangerous
But together they exert great power
In the Gorge
The Columbia River Gorge
We stand in awe of it
We harness it best we can
By writing
Painting
Carving
All types of creative powers are
Set free here in the Gorge

The Mount Hood dance

When the sun is shinning
The mountain stands crystal clear
So sharp and crisp above all the mist
But on a cloudy windy day
The mountain can still be seen
The winter wind is blowing
The clouds are floating by
Doing a dance across and over
The mountain on a cloudy windy day
It looks like the mountain is doing
A winter dance
A dance to honor all the
All those left for lost
On the snowy snowy cliffs
All those who tried and failed
To scale the mountains sides
All those souls still lingering
On the mountains ground

The night belongs to me
Rev 07/ 2018

The moon is not full
But shinning on the mountain
The sky is not clear
But the clouds spotty
Around the mountain
The air is not freezing
But not yet warm in the evening
It will rain a bit tonight
But not for now
I stand here taking in the sight
Of the mountain moving in and out
Of the clouds
The rays of the moon light up the sky
And the side of the mountain
Seems like there is no one
Left in the world tonight
All this show is just for me
As everyone else is gone
Gone to sleep land
A land so far away
But for now the Gorge is here
Only for me
I will soak it all in
For the night
Belongs to me

The lady in red
I feel so sexy
They stop and stare
A few dare to touch
Some tell me things
When no one else can hear
I feel so naked
The wind blows through me
As I stand on the street
I am not ashamed
So stare at me please
I feel so trapped
I cannot turn to the water
I cannot run across the street
I would love to follow them home
I would love to sit for a spell
I feel so tall
On my pedestal they place me
To see above all

Tiny Tiny Town (rev 02/2018)

I live in a tiny tiny town
Where did all this traffic come from
Used to be at nine and five be three or four
And we'd all be fine
Come Friday night the wind surfers come
We love their money and love their women
Riding the river makes them happy
Their happy we happy everybody happy
Makes me happy on Sunday night when they have gone

I live in a tiny tiny town
Where did all this traffic come from
On Saturday night I like to go on down
Down to the TarWater for a beer
Still know most of everyone
I like it when the new girls come in
I like the one with the curly hair
I think I might take her home tonight
She's so cute and she's so sweet
She just might be the one for me
But if she's not we'll just have some fun
And maybe we'll meet again real soon

I live in a tiny tiny town
Where did all this traffic come from
On Sunday morn I don't go
I stay home and pray like everyday
I smoke a little pot and drink a little beer
The law don't like me and I don't care
Me and Gods good so I'm ok
I know I'm here to stay

I live in a tiny tiny town
Where did all this traffic come from
Won't be long and you'll be putting me in the ground
Don't you worry I just moved a little
A little south west of where Jesus lives
He has a big house I have a small house
But it's bigger than my old house
But it's ok I come from a tiny tiny town
Now I live in a tiny tiny town
That has no traffic at all

Walking down (rev 02/2018)

Walking down walking down to the Tarwater
Going to drink cold whisky at the Tarwater
At the Tarwater…tonight
Going to smoke a bowl
Before I go
Before walking down
Down to the Tarwater
The Tarwater tonight
The sunset is down
And the mountain is up
What a beautiful site
With the mountain and the river
And the moon shinning on it
All on the walk down
To the Tarwater tonight
Don't know who will be there tonight
Don't know who's tending tonight
Don't matter much as
All the bartenders
Are cute and so nice
Don't know who will be there tonight
Maybe a little cutie or maybe
Someone interesting
All at the Tarwater
Tonight
When it's over
Time for me to go home
I'll be walking back

Back from the Tarwater
Tonight

Down below
The sound of the train sprang up the hill
The rumble as the train runs along the river
The whistle so shrill as it passed through the town below
All sounds are just a mile away
But sound so close to us
This is a new town for my dogs and I
The dogs have grown accustomed
To the sounds of a new neighborhood
But the one sound that still puzzles them
Is the sound of the train
They hear the rumble before the train sounds
Its whistle for the street crossing outside of town
And when the whistle blows they perk up their ears
And lift their heads wherever they are
Be it asleep or eating or out in the yard
They stop and listen with wonder on their little faces
I am tempted to take them down the hill and sit by the tracks
One day until a train goes by
Just so they can see what it is that makes that noise

Coffee
07/2018

Coffee what a blessing you are
Coffee you taste as luxury would taste
Coffee you make me feel alive when I wish I was not
Coffee you make me feel awake though I am not
Coffee your aroma makes me want to wake even earlier
Coffee you make me so happy
Coffee make me laugh but please don't spill on my white shirt
Even cold you make me smile at my stained shirt
Good thing I live in a small town

The autumn chill (rev 02/0218)

When the autumn chill takes over the night
You don your hoodie you pull on some shoes
Or boots
Go for your walk in the night
The brisk air is not so cold yet to sting
Your face heats quickly
Your hands not numb but getting stiff
You shove them into your pocket
And vow to get the gloves out tomorrow
Less people now
Less tourist staying in town
More when the snow falls in the mountains
But now is a quiet time for us
Dogs most inside
I pass on by and mean no harm to them
Or theirs
If my dogs are with me they travel
Silently make no noise do not respond
Occasionally I see deer raccoons or a coyote or two
Wild life know danger
And know when someone
Is just moving through the night
Like they move through the night
We both stop and stare and then move off
But it is my demons that I seek to cage
When I walk at night
A chance to lock them up for the night

So I may have a good night's sleep

Just a stone's throw away
The mighty Columbia flows
Just a stone's throw away
Mount Hood is over the hill
Just a stone's throw away
Mount Adams not much further
Just a stone's throw away
The hills of Horse Heaven
Around the bend
Just a stone's throw away
Welcome to the West Gorge of the
Columbia River where
So much is
Just a stone's throw away

Love the Gorge (rev 02/2018)

I live in the Columbia River Gorge
The river itself is thing of power and beauty
Views of not just the river
But of Mount Hood
And Mount Adams
Abound
Other rivers flow into the Columbia
From both sides of her shores
Lakes throughout the region
Wild life everywhere you go
From river fowl
To deer and predators
The rivers and lakes still
Home to many a fish
But above all else in the Gorge
The site most common
The site most beautiful
Are the women of
The Columbia River Gorge
As in nary a land will
You see such beauty as thee

Cliff dwellers

As I stood on the rivers banks
On the north side
I look high into the sky to the north
And there all along the edge
Of the cliffs above
Are all the million-dollar homes
Lined up on cliffs edge
It seems as though just a little shake
And they all will come tumbling down
They are so high up that you can barely
See the decks hanging out in space
Too far to see a person on the deck
Or in a window
But they look out their windows or come
Out on their decks on occasion
Or why spend all that money for that view
If you never pay any attention to it

The cold
Rev 07/2018

When the cold bites
At your skin
Seeps through you jeans
And chills your legs
When the wind
Blows through
The jacket zipper
And causes you to take
A deep breath
When the wind dry's
All the moisture in your eyes
If you stop walking you feel
The cold seeping through
The boots and socks
To your feet
This is winter in the Gorge
The Columbia River Gorge

A love poem
07/2018
I sit on my truck
At the top of the hill
I can almost see
Idaho
In the east
And to the west
Portland
Not quite almost
To the south her royal majesty
Mount Hood
Standing like a queen
Viewing all of her kingdom
This is life in the Columbia Gorge
Whatever else happens
I hope to stay here till I die
Maybe you will come and visit
Maybe you might stay
With me for a spell
Maybe we can write some poems
Or songs together
And just enjoy this splendor

A trip to The Dalles
I love driving east from Bengin
Down the Gorge
I normally drive down 14
Just cause there's no toll
It's so cool to see the green
Turn to brown as you travel along
As you move into eastern WA
Pass by Lyle a quiet little burg
But has a bar so....
On past names with not much on the highway
Till you get to the dam and the highway crosses
To the Dalles
Spread out down the river
The hospital and medical clinics all
Along the top of the ridge overlooking all
The only Fred Myers in miles around
Pretty much where ever you are in the Dalles
If you face towards the river you see the water
And red and brown bluffs that crisscross
The landscape
A sight well worth the drive from here
And a chance to shop at a Fred Myers

The river
07/ 2018

There is a saying in the Gorge
That the river washes away the sins
Of the people on the river
Turns out that many
River communities have similar expressions
As the rivers carry the dumped waste
The industrial toxins
The things people and companies
Just dump so they are not on the hook
For disposing responsibly
Then there are the other sins
Which are washed down river
Someone's spouse who suddenly
Leaves town never to return

Barely

The river is so like glass
With the barge
Being pulled down the river
Barely a ripple
Barely a breeze on the surface
No caps to show the white
Only the ripples out from the barge
As it passes by

Another night in White Salmon
I love sitting on the deck at night
And listen to the quiet
Every sound
Stands out so distinctly
The sound of a car on Estes
The sound of the train
Rolling through Bingen
A siren in Hood River
A plane crosses the Gorge
A night walker strolls down the alley
Almost soundless
But I can see the shadow
Cross the streetlamp in the back
A possum scurries up the street
A bat cuts across the
The neighbor's porch light
White Salmon at night
Is peaceful
But much more goes on
Than you might think
Late at night

The river
(rev 02/2018)

The river flows
The surface so smooth
Nary a ripple from a distance
It seems to be like a standing pond
And yet just below the eye
The undercurrent moves with one mind
To reach the ocean to find the tides
To bind with that body of water
That calls to the river from the depths of the ocean
To the highest mountain top
Come to me
Flow into me
And I will take you in
You will become a part something bigger
There is nothing larger
More powerful than the Columbia River
Till you get to the Pacific Ocean

The Hill
(rev 02/2018
The walk home from the bar
The sky so full of stars
The hill so steep
The ground so rutted
I walk home alone again
Maybe there is hope
On the horizon
Or maybe you will always
Walk this hill alone
But turn around
And in the moonlight you can see
Mount Hood against the moon
Alone or not this is now my home
No other place like it in the entire world
White Salmon

Smoke in the Gorge
(rev 2/ 2018)

When you look out at it
It looks like fog
But when you step out
The burning in your lungs
The sting in your eyes
Tells you it is smoke
Smoke from a forest fire
When you walk down the street
Whiffs of smoke drift past you
All around you
All over you
When you step inside the smell stays with you
Until you change your cloths
Take a shower and scrub your skin
Day after day night after night
The sun and moon both red as your blood
You pray for rain to wash the air
To douse the flames
To relieve those that dedicate
Their lives to fighting these fires
And to clear your senses of the harsh smell
Of the smoke

Watching the Columbia River
(rev 2/2018)

Watching the Columbia River
As it
Pours its way down the Gorge
I wonder what happens
To a molecule of water in the river
How long does it take to get
To the mouth
Does it take a few days or weeks
Or is it years or decades if it ends up along the shore
Watching the Columbia River
As it
Flows down the Gorge to
The ocean eagerly waiting
All the molecules of water
To be added to the ocean

I shot you in the head
What do you think
I thought of you
When I stepped over your dead body
And didn't even look down
You got so loud
And yelled all the time
And the dirty looks
Were just more than I could take
So one morning
I shoot you in the head
I stepped over your body
And didn't feel bad at all
Dumped you in the river
Tied to a cement block
Don't think you'll be back again
And sure won't be yelling much
No one else knows or cares
That you're not around anymore
Don't except no CSI's
To come to the door
I doubt they care either
Long as you don't wash ashore
I think this is all but done
And no one cares anymore

So I'm going find me
A new girlfriend
One that is sweet
Never raises her voice
And has such a nice look on her face

Nice little town
(rev 2/2018)

Such a nice little town
Such a quiet little town
Don't get to know your neighbor
Till the fall comes around

Such nice little town
Such a quiet little town
All autumn long
We all hang around

Such a nice little town
Such a quiet little town
All winter long
We all huddle up to stay warm

Such a nice little town
Such a quiet little town
All spring long
We all clean the town

Such a nice little town
Such a quiet little town
Then the summer comes around
And the tourists come to town

Such a nice little town
Such a quiet little town
All year round we enjoy
Our little town

Hot days cool nights

Cruising down 14
In the middle of the night
Been a hot day all day long
But it's a cool cool night tonight
Nowhere to be headed somewhere

Cruising down 14
In the middle of the night
Got the window rolled down
Wind in my face
Going a steady pace

Cruising down 14
In the middle of the night
Feels so nice just to be free
Not penned up anymore today
Changed my mind going a little further

Cruising down 14
In the middle of the night
If I had a love sitting by my side
We would head up to Underwood
And take in the sight

Cruising down 14
In the middle of the night
The sun starting to rise
And it's time to get some rest

Headed home for some sleep and a new day

Autumn coming to the Gorge
Rev 02/2018

The chill is coming back into the air
It is still hot to warm during the day
The sun begins setting earlier everyday
And the leaves are being touched by color
The tomatoes are turning red with urgency
As they seem to know the days are limited
Until they will be bitten by the frost
The windsurfers are as frantic
As the tomatoes
But they are looking for winds
Fire fighters looking for the rains
For relief from the summer fires
This the beginning of autumn in the Gorge
The Columbia River Gorge

Another song about the wind
Rev 02/2018

The wind has come to visit the Gorge
It never stays to long
It just blows on in and blows on by
Blows up the dust
And forest fire soot from the street
And off the leaves of all the trees

The wind has come to visit the Gorge
It never stays to long
It just blows on in and blows on by
Don't take it personal that the wind doesn't stay
It just comes
And goes as it pleases

The wind has come to visit the Gorge
It never stays to long
It just blows on in and blows on by
Once asked it why as it blew by
All I got was dust in the eye
As it blew by

Rev 02/2018
The wind so still
The water so smooth
If you stand in the same place every night
It's a different view
Is the moon out
Are there clouds
Is there a wind
From what direction
Has it rained
Is it snowing
Is it foggy
Barges or paddle boats out tonight
Foggy or smoky
They all change the view
Each night anew

You will know my name if only for a moment
The wind in the Gorge blows right past you
The wind in the Gorge cares not your name
Your fame
You're rich or poor
It just blows right past you
From the west it blows from the ocean cool
In the summer
Warm in the winter
And sometimes wet
It blows up the river
The river protests and white caps appear
From the east it blows off the deserts
Hot in the summer
Freezing cold in the winter
Down the Gorge along the river flow
The river cares not that the east wind blows
The wind in the Gorge blows right past you
The wind in the Gorge cares not your name
I stand with my face into the wind
I cry my name out
You will know my name if only for a
Moment
As the wind on the Gorge blows past me

Up and down the river
Rev 02/2018

Up and down the river
They toil all day
Up and down the river
They run all night
Pushing or pulling
A ship or a barge
It matters not too a tug
Just get them up or
Get them down
Up or down the river
Day or night up or down
It matters not to a tug
Up and down the river
They toil all day
Up and down the river
They run all night
They silhouette the water
In the night
Lights all a bright and shadows cast
Up and down the river
They run all night
It matters not to a tug

The battle of Eagle Creek
The roar of the flame
So close getting closer
The smoke so thick
We can't see the flame
Only hear it moving towards us
We are digging trenches
Falling trees to create a break
Will we finish in time
The plane passes overhead
The load is dumped on the fire
It quiets for a few minutes
We know it won't last long
Before it is on the move again
 Even with the mask and oxygen
The smoke burns the eyes and lungs
But if we don't finish this break
Before the flames are on us
We will have to pull the blankets
Over us we are seasoned fighters
We have done this before
The roar of the flame so much closer
The plane is dropping another load
It will buy us few more minutes
A chance to stop this beast
From all of us here in the Gorge to all of
You who fought the fires
God bless, and protect you and your families
Thank you

Autumn in the Columbia Gorge 2017
(rev 02/2018

The rain is washing the smoke from the air
It is clean again
We can see the scars from the summer fires
To the south across the river
On the cliffs and hillsides
Some still smoldering smoke rising up
Autumn will be dangerous this year
The scars are new paths for the rainwater
To come crashing down
Mud and rock slides
Instead of autumn colors to see
We will watch for flash floods
The ground has lost its anchors
There will be more homes lost to the slides
Than the fires took
Odds are high there will be lives lost
As unlike fires
Flash floods give little warning
This year the fall colors will be different
Huge swaths of forest have been burned out
Next spring a new color pallet will be showing
As the scars will be populated with
The wildflowers
Saplings and seedlings
New colors for next autumns
Color scheme
As the Gorge works to heal itself

Fire season

Been dry for weeks
Now the forest fires
Are burning throughout the land
The acid smoke is heavy in the air
When you walk on the street at night
With the flashlight pointed to the ground
You can see the ash stirring on the ground
From your footsteps
Look behind you and you can see the trail
From your footsteps
If only I could look ahead
And see footsteps
Footsteps to follow to my next
Adventure or off the edge of a cliff
But no footsteps are ahead of me
And as the breeze picks up
There are none behind me now
My life my past is gone can never be returned to
My future uncertain at best
But what is that I feel on my face
A rain drop
Now another
The fire season could be drawing to a close
I hope so it's hard to see ahead in the smoky air
And being able to see in front of me
Is really important right now

Quite a delight

Seeing the Columbia River at night
Is to be believed only by your eyes
Seeing the Columbia River at night
Is really quite a delight

Seeing the moonlight bounce off the water
Seeing the stars all dancing in the sky
Seeing the Colombia River at night
Is really quite a delight

Don't just drive on by
Stop and take it all in
As one never knows when you will see
The Colombia River at night ...again

All winter long in White Salmon
Rev 02/2018

All winter long
It's such a quiet little town
Such a pretty little town
Sitting on the cliff
All on its own

Summer comes along
And it gets so warm
The tourists come along
 Just to have some fun
On rivers and the trails

All summer long
They hurry along
They laugh at us who
Live in this quiet little town
And they keep us in cash

They are always on the dash
Wanting to eat wanting to hike
Wanting to party
So much want is what keeps us going
All winter long

When the winter comes
Some still come around
Quieter now
Locals coming out
Our pretty little town

All winter long
It's such a quiet little town
Such a pretty little town
Sitting on the cliff
All on its own

The morning so clear

Just another day
But like all days
Things to be noticed
If your eyes are open
The mountain so clear but one
Low hanging cloud across the center
Of Mount Hood
The sun so bright
And so warm for May
The river so high
The islands all submerged
The traffic is still light
But there are tourists in the grocery
The season will be on us soon
But remember this day
Not for the tourist
But for the cloud
The sun bright and warm
The river so high
These are things I will remember this day by

Second Hand Rose
Rev 02/2018
Second Hand Rose
Is a thrift store in Bingen
I go there and buy my clothes
One dollar for tees
Three dollars for shirts
And sweat shirts for four
Like five dollars for a pair of pants
It fits my budget and it fits my taste
These days
But what I really enjoy
Is all the odd stuff
The kitchen utensils
The ceramic animals and knick knacks
The games and stuff from times gone past
But still showing up in people's closets
Some look like new others bare
With use and age
You wonder what the difference was
From one home to another
That caused this set of silverware to be so dinged
And another set looks like new
The golf clubs…well we can understand
Why the difference there
To see the flower vase so worn and stained
We know how the unused one got to the thrift shop

The board games always interest me what was it like
In the house that played all the time
Opposed to the one that still has pieces
In plastic
Maybe it balances out with the electronics
The old systems barely held together
With games looking very suspect in condition
Maybe the family who never played board games
Played electronics
So there is the game I play at
Second Hands Roses
So when you hit Bingen on 14
Don't drive through
Stop have lunch
And visit Second Hand Rose
And find a treasure for you

The Columbia River
Rev 02/2018
So powerful a force
That can be slowed
Can be diverted
But cannot be stopped
It flows constantly
Never stopping
So much energy is harnessed
From this river
But watch it closely
As it seems to be very resentful
Always looking for a way around
For a way over or under
If all else fails she pushes constantly
To go through whatever is blocking her
One lose brick one mistake
And this river will destroy
Everything is its wake

Cold Toenails

My feet are so cold
Even my toenails are cold
My hands half numb
I put up my hood
In bed
To keep my head warm
Welcome to life with a pellet stove
As heat
In the winter of 2016
In the gorge

The Hood
Rev 02/2018

Welcome to the hood
The Hood River hood
With views of the Columbia
With Mount Hood to the south
And Mount Adams to the North
Where a drive down Walnut takes a half hour
Due to all the people crossing the street
The homes on the hill
Fit the bill in the early 1900s
The breweries in town are quite the attraction
And gets the attention of all who pass
And the bridge across the Columbia cost a dollar
Now two dollars
Two dollars to Washington two dollars to Oregon
Across the great Columbia you go for two bucks
There is no mall there is no Costco
Welcome to the hood
The Hood River hood
And the cutest girl in the local artist co-op
Wind surfing shops at every corner
Hotels on the river covered in wind surfers
But bring your own bags to the stores
Or you're carrying your stuff out in your pockets
Welcome to the hood
The Hood River hood

Wind on the move (rev 02/2018)

The wind blows across the mountains
From where it's been no one knows
Who knows what it has seen
The wind blows through my hair
From where it's been who knows what it has touched
Or who else it has touched
Who knows what it will see as it blows on
Who knows who else it will touch as it blows by
To know what the wind knows
To know who the wind knows
To travel so freely to see what you wish
To be so close to so many
To be there so briefly
And be able to leave at your will
To blow across the mountains
To blow through some one's hair

Home today

I look out my window
Nothing has changed
Throughout the day
I walk down the street
Look down the hill
To downtown
I look up to the east to the foot hills
That begins eastern Washington
I look to the south east across the river
To the foot hills
That begins eastern Oregon
I look to the south to Mount Hood
So tall and powerful
I look past the downtown
To the Columbia River flowing
On its journey to the sea
Too far to see the sea but close enough
For its winds to blow cool air
In the summer
And to blow warm air
In the winter
This is now my home
I did not start here
I am not sure why I am here
But here is where God sent me
So until he says otherwise
I will stay watching the river flow by
Under the mountain so high

The Drive from Lynnwood to White Salmon
Rev 02/2018

It's a boring boring drive from Lynnwood too White Salmon
And if your heart is broken it is long long trip
If you hit Tacoma within an hour you'll make White Salmon in four or five
I hate that stretch between Tacoma and Olympia
If it wasn't for my tears I would see how boring boring it is

It's a boring boring drive from Lynnwood too White Salmon
If you hit fourteen in three you can make White Salmon in four
Along fourteen to White Salmon is very nice trip
If my tears have cleared enough to see the scenery
When you get to the bottom where Bengin lays
Just turn left and go up the hill
For in White Salmon they have three bars to welcome you to town

I know where I'm going in White Salmon but I
don't know where I'll be
Nor how long I'll be in White Salmon
That depends on finding a girl friend or two
Always wanted two to take care of me maybe
now's the time
But I think you can count on me not making that
Boring boring drive from White Salmon too
Lynnwood to many more times

The changing season in White Salmon
Rev 02/2018

The days are still hot in the afternoons
But now they end with a cool evening
And chill in the morning
I love standing on the deck
When inside is hot and stuffy
But the cool breeze has begun
It feels so good
It blows out all of the days sweat and frustrations
Carries the promise of the night with it
The promise of new adventures
New people to meet
New stories to hear told
To laugh out loud
Perchance to dance blindly hearing only the music
And seeing only her
The chill of the evening when you walk home
The warmth of her in your arms as your lips find hers
The seasons change it becomes warmer or cooler
The seasons of love change as well
From year to year old loves new loves no love
So it goes
So goes the season changing now
In White Salmon

The Washington Side

When I'm a driving down the Columbia River Gorge
I like to drive on the Washington side
The rides a little bumpy and a little bit lumpy
And there are a lot of stops and too many cops
The roads a little curvy and can be a bit nervy
But I like driving on the Washington side

When I'm a driving down the Columbia River Gorge
I like to drive on the Washington side
If it's a little sunny and a little windy
There are windsurfers all about
All about the roads and all about the river
All about the bars and all about the parks
All about the Columbia River Gorge

When I'm a driving down the Columbia River Gorge
I like to drive on the Washington side
The highway runs all along the shore
If you riding high you're looking down the cliff
Keep your eyes on the road if you're driving
Down the Columbia River Gorge

When I'm a driving down the Columbia River Gorge
I like to drive on the Washington side
When you get to Bingen stop at Beneventi's
And have pizza and a salad bar
If you want a beer just drive-up the hill
White Salmon has a brewery and the best-looking girls
In the Columbia River Gorge

When I'm a driving down the Columbia River Gorge
I like to drive on the Washington side

Pretty Girl in the Store
I am walking through the Thriftway
In White Salmon
Not a care in the world
I see you down the isle
Picking out your island soap
You're so cute you're so hot
You're so innocent and so not
What do I say and still stay cool
I don't want to get slapped
Or arrested or laughed at
If I had your number I would text you
Let's go out to dinner
If I had your email I would email you
And ask you out to coffee
If I knew your kirk or your Instagram
Or maybe your tweet
 I would if I could
Tell you of my new-found love
For you
Pretty girl in the store

White Salmon

I came here to heal
And heal I shall
In the crisp winter air
Overlooking the Columbia River
Under the watch of Mount Hood
Here in White Salmon
I came here to heal
And heal I shall
My soul will have the scars
My face the added lines
But my mind will be right
My goals changed but goals I will have
I came here to heal
And healing I am
Here in White Salmon
Spring will be here before long
The air will begin to warm
The sun will shine again
I will be healed by then
Here in White Salmon
I will make my home

Sunset over the Gorge
Rev (02/2018)

As the light shines out
Of the clouds
At the end of day
Lighting up the river
The walls of the Gorge
The bridge casting a shadow
On to the river
How long does a sunset last
Five minutes ten
Never counted it myself
Maybe one day
But for now I will just enjoy it
And watch as the darkness
Takes over and sets in for the night
The night is my time
And the stars are my company
For the night
The moon my light by which to walk
Till the light of day returns
To the Gorge

Walking the stormy streets
The water runs down the street
The leaves blow past
Riding the gust of wind to the end
The branches sway to and fro
The slim trees bend at middle
The large trees stand stoic with only
The upper branches whipping
Only at the ends
The wind so gusty so busty
Through all the Gorge tonight
Reaching through my jacket
To chill me to the bone
Time to find the path home

Walking

Walking on a sunny day
Walking on a small-town street
Walking on a sunny day
Oh what a treat

Walking on a small-town street
Just listening to my own beat
Never thinking about the next step
Just walking on a small-town street

Just listening to my own beat
Not worrying about anything
Walking on a small-town street
Never thought I would be here

Not worrying about a thing
Saying hello to all I meet
Just walking on a small-town street
Love living in a small town

Love walking on a small-town street
Don't meet any I don't know
And if do
I know them now

Walking on a small-town street
Headed back to the house
Going to sit on the deck
And write a little song

About walking down
A small-town street

Windy day (02/2018)
Wind blowing against the glass
Wind blowing across the grass
Rain pouring off the roof
Right down my neck
Tis a day we will not go a walking
Best spend the day
A texting
Start a fire in the fireplace
Warm those feet
From the coals
As the time for bed
Rolls around
Power is out
Sleep on floor
Next to the fireplace
Nights are cold in the Gorge
Wear socks to bed

Start to finish
Rev 02/2018
It starts with a drip
From a snow bank
High in the mountains
Of Canada
It ends at the mouth
Of the Columbia River
And here is the rest of the story
A million billion drips in the mountains
A thousand creeks down
The ravines
All come together in the valleys
For hundreds of streams
Down the hills
To form the rivers below
Hundreds of other rivers
Flow into this one so large
Now it is the Columbia
And well on and on to the Gorge
There are dams and obstacles
Along the way
But the river just keeps pushing ahead
The barges and paddle boats
Maneuver along its surface
The fish swim up or down
Depending on the order of the day
But there is no way that the river
Will be delayed

From delivering its contents to the Ocean

Just another day
Traveling across the Columbia
On a sunny day
On the Hood River bridge
Is a treat
I look forward to days
Where there is construction
So I stop and look out
You can tell the water level
By how much of the little islands
Are showing above the water
If the wind is from the west
The water is choppy
From the east smooth
The tug boats with their
Barges they have for the day
Filled with lumber
Or wheat
Coming from the east
To the mills and processors
In the west
The wind surfers on the water
The temperature of the day matters
Little to them as they all wear wet suits
Always something going on
On the Columbia River

The river is so quiet
When you sit next to a brook
Or a stream even a small river
You hear the rush of the water
The sound of water flowing off the
Partially submerged stones and logs
A small river has a roar to it as it flows
So swiftly past
But the Columbia is no small anything
In most places it looks placid and harmless
But throw a piece of driftwood out
And see it pulled under the water
By the currents to bob up several yards
Downriver without ever making a sound
This is a silent giant stealthy marching
To its destination in Astoria
There are exceptions along the course
Of the Columbia
When it flows through the vents and by ways
Of the dams this is an angry river
And the roar is one you will not soon forget
As the river vows to break these dams one day
And flow free as it had for millions of years

A tributary

All you can hear
Is the water flowing
And falling off a cliff
All you can see
Is the darkness
With splashes of light
Hitting the water
As it flows by
Into the night
Off the cliff
And down the hill
Only a short mile
And this stream
Will join the Columbia
For its march

The Columbia on a moonlit night

When the moon is out
I love to find a place to watch the river
The moon on the water
On a still night
My chest gets tight
Breathing is more difficult
It feels primitive
Something stirs within me
I feel like putting my nose into the air
Singing a song of being alone
Dancing a dance
To somehow cause ripples
On that water
Somehow I feel I could lift a boulder
I feel like I could swim that river
My dance is filled with lust and power
Physical power and my brain alive
With instinct
Simplicity
I am aroused
I am primed for something
Something I have never identified
But I am always careful
To be sure no one is around
When I visit the river
On a moonlit night

Morning in White Salmon

The sun is just on the horizon
The clouds from the night before
Are blowing down the Gorge
The mountain is so clear like a picture
Hanging across the sky with the
Red of the morning on its side
The river has a mist
Running all down the shore
Tug boat captains standing on the deck
Stretching out the nights work
And opening their eyes to a new day
The deer move to higher ground
To avoid the traffic of the day
And the barking of the morning dogs
High school kids racing
To get to class
Workers headed out across the bridge
Or down 14 to the Dallas
Soon all will be quiet
And I can take the dogs for a walk
I love White Salmon in the mornings
When the sun comes up warm

Waters Journey

How does a water fall freeze
Does it start at the bottom
And freeze upward or
Does start at the top and freeze downward
However it happens it is surreal to see
A frozen waterfall
With no water flowing
All suspended in space
Frozen on its journey
To the river to the ocean
To watch another day
As the water begins to flow
Flowing down the ice to the low ground
Flowing across the frozen pond or stream
Soon no ice remains just the flowing water
On its way to the river to the ocean

Hottest Bartender in Town
She is the hottest bartender in the town
Everyone is in love with her
But it is a small town
Take away the gay guys who just want to hang
And you deduct the married men as she has morals
Take out those who don't have the means to support themselves
Much less her and her daughter
Take out the ones in and out of jail
The addicts and the abusive dicks
The ones that are here for just the summer kicks
Those who are too ugly or fat to be contenders
Eliminate the ones that are too old
Where does that leave her
Well there is a guy that is courting constantly
Who owns his business and talks a lot
There is the guy who brings her dinner at the bar
Who never says much of anything
So with her daughter she lives alone
She does not seem unhappy about it
But I suspect she is lonely
Someday her prince will come along
Someone good for her and the daughter
She will still be the hottest bartender in the town

Summer afternoon

The day was so sunny
And so warm
But on the river the breeze swept by
In spurts
Warm and still one moment
Cool and breezy the next
We walked on the beach
I skipped rocks
You found rocks to take home
I held you hand as we stepped on the stones
I looked in your eyes as we spoke
We laughed and petted someone's dog
A day I will remember to the end of my time
And if I can beyond

Closing time
Wondering off into the night
As the bar closes till tomorrow
No hurry no push up the hill
I climb
Another night done
Another trip home
The air so fresh the spring chill still
Hangs onto the night
I watch for the regular night folks
To see who is still moving around
The tv on in the house across from the park
The high school kids still partying
In their garage
The neighbor who reads by flash light
On his porch
And of course the guy who walks home from the bar

Sunday night at the Tarwater

Another night at the Tarwater
A Sunday night
All regulars not busy
But the bar is full
After I take the last spot
Lots of laughter
Stories going back and forth
I weight in as these are
As close to friends as I have these days
Bar friends
I am happy to have them
To joke for a spell
To hear a story here and there
I don't stay long these days
Just two or three and I am on my way
Back up the hill
Better this way I don't risk
Showing too much of me
My anger
My loneliness
My fear
My hurt
Time to climb the hill once again
Alone my heart is heavier than my legs
At the top of the hill

I breathe deep into the air
I went out tonight
Did nothing to be ashamed of
It has been a good night

Down to the river tonight

I'm going down to the river tonight
I'm going to drown
Every memory I have of you
I'm going hold them under the water
Till they stop haunting me
I'm going to watch them float down the river
On the current
To the sea
And away from both you and me
I'm going down to the river tonight
I'm going to wash myself
Clean of every memory
I'm going to hold my head under the water
Till there is no memory of you left in me
I am going float them down the river
To the sea and neither you or I
Will ever find them again
I'm down to the river tonight
Laying on the bank like an empty shell
But all my memories of you
Are gone
But tomorrow when I wake
They'll be back in my mind
And by evening
I will go down to the river again

Hop on down to the Tarwater
A happening place to be
People all over the
Place
You're bound to have fun tonight

Bet you will have a good time
In whatever mood you are in
Rolling down the hill
To the Tarwater
Hell a place to be
Dance on in
Ahead of the crowd
You'll have a good seat

Sitting on the river bank
Sitting on the shore
So cute
Such a lovely smile
But it was the laugh
That caught my attention
Before I could see you
The laugh so soft
Yet I could hear it
Several yards away
So real no doubt
It was a true laugh
But you were with a group
Who knows the relations
Or not
But all I could do was glance
And smile as I walked past
And you
Never to be seen again

Walking hanging kissing driving
Walking not running
Walking not running
All the way down the street
With my baby

Hanging
Hanging
Hanging on my arm
All the way down the hill

We're kissing
Kissing
Kissing in the coffee shop
Kissing in the coffee shop doorway

We're driving
Driving
Driving not to far
Just to the cliff for some more

Kissing
Kissing
Kissing in the car
We're kissing in the car on the cliff

Brrr

The wind is blowing
Tonight
And it tis a cold cold night
The wind cuts through the jacket
Without mercy
The cold has no soul
And freezes one to the bone

Snow

The snow falls takes over the landscape
As the temperatures stay low
The snow flies mostly at night
And builds and controls all that you see
But when the temperatures begin to rise
The snow starts to drop off the trees
A little rain comes one night
And the control over the land
Is relented
Snow cover
Become islands of snow
Then just blotches
Then just the parking lot snow pile remain
And the land returns to itself

Sometimes... just for a moment
Walking down the hill
With a strut in my step
Going out for a spell
Down at the Tarwater
Not a late night
As got prose wanting out
But such lively steps all down the hill
Have cold whiskey maybe two
Met a nice woman
About a half hour in
I flirted my best got her to smile and chat
Just for a bit
But
Off she goes as all they must
Such a nice touch on my arm as she left
I may never see her again
But I will remember you for all that's left
As that touch on the arm just for a bit
Will write poems and lyrics
About that touch on the arm
The smile and chat
So cash out my tab and back up the hill
No strut left no lively in my step
Just a trudge up that hill
But the truth is when I get there I will
Write a little ditty bout this trip to the Tarwater
And that touch on the arm so long missed

The estate sale on Oak street

It is hard sometimes to find
People you really like and can bond with
So when you find one it's...cool
The other day I went to an estate sale
Just down the street from where I live
While walking through the house I began
To realize this man took care of his stuff
Things are clean a lot of stuff still had
The original boxes for storing
He liked his coats lots of cool jackets
Lots of garden stuff not just tools
But yard art as well
I loved the taste for wall hangings
A lot of small very quality pieces of art
And furniture, even the kitchen things
Spoke of someone who appreciated what they had
It appears the wife passed first
Mostly men's clothing
The woman's things were in a room
Being stored
This was their home and looked like
They had lived here a long time
Then she passed
Did she get sick or was there an accident
Probably an illness a cancer of some sort
And he stayed on in their home
Long enough to have given away her stuff
Except things like her wedding dress

Some of her jackets probably the favorites
And he stayed in this house
Never remarried
I suspect he lived as full of a life as possible
But always he was bidding his time
To join her
I wish I had known them or at least him after his loss
I believe he had character and soul
He would have been an interesting friend to have
But now they are happy
To be back in each other's arms
God bless you sir
I cried at your estate sale

Sunny day

Sitting on the step
On a sunny day
Don't know which way
I'll go today
Don't know if
I'll go at all
Don't know what
I want
Or what I want to do
At least not today
As I am
Sitting on the step
On a sunny day
Maybe I'll move
Later on today
Maybe I'll just sit
For the rest of the day
Smoke a joint
Stay for a while
As I am
Sitting on the step
On a sunny day
Getting high
And not thinking of much
Of anything
Just thinking of
All the things
I will write later today

As I am
Sitting on the step
On a sunny day

Up through the dirt

Late winter I start searching the ground
Looking for those signs of life returning
From the year before
Little green shoots pushing up
Through the dirt
Shoots from bulbs and perennials
Little red stems of peonies
Peeking back up at me from the dirt
Life life how I love the life
That comes back every year
To sway with joy to the wind
Lean into the sun with such eagerness
Push the buds out bursting with flowers
Rich with color and scents for the bees
And for our noses
Filled with pollen and seeds
To begin new lives again and again

End of the day in the Gorge
The burning sears
Across the landscape
The hillsides ablaze
The mountain side bleeding
Down the slopes
The river a fire with the
Reflections of all that
Is above it
A beautiful day in the Gorge
ends with
Sunset

Just a day in the Gorge
Clouds blowing by
All through the sky
Rain in the hills and mountains
Flow down from the hills on high
To flow with the Columbia
Down the Gorge to the sea
People travel up and down
The river banks
84 and 14 east and west
Highways never take a rest
Every glance into the sky
Reveals a bird of prey on high
Fish swim up and down
Depending on the cycle
Boats and barges
Flow like the fish
Depending on
The time of the year
Windsurfers haunt
White caps off Hood River
Above it all Mount Hood
Presides
Guided by God alone
Just a day in the Gorge

Tell the boss you need another week
Let's just take a moment
I understand how this works
Did myself most of my life
Hurry here and hurry there
Only have a week off
Then back to the grind
Got to make the hotel by six
Or they give our room up
To someone else
No more stops between
Here and there
Got go get a move on
Only have a week off
Must make the most of it
But let's just stop
Get out of the car
Feel the soil under your feet
See the sky above your head
See the mountains off not so far
See the river flowing
Across your vision
See the barges flowing by
See the birds in the sky
Feel the breeze on your face
The sun so warm on your back
Call the office tell them
You're taking another week
In the Gorge

New friends
Sitting in the library
Surrounded by people
People I don't really know
Reading for the first time
One of my poems
Out loud
Never done this before
Not sure
How I feel about it yet

Art ...Gods power in human kind
I live in the Columbia Gorge
The Gorge is filled with artist
Writers
Poets
Musicians
Painters
And on and on
Everywhere you look
The river
The mountain
God's creations
Of beauty and power
Pull out the real people
Within us
The power is palatable
I feel it now as I write
The need to create
The drive to write
Thank you Lord

Walking on down

I am walking on down
To the Tarwater tonight
Going to light one on
At the Tarwater tonight
Going to talk to every
Cute girl I can
See if one talks back
Make her smile if I can
I am walking on down
To the Tarwater tonight
Going see if I can find me a girl
Not just one for the night
But one till the end of my days
Long shot in a bar
But you never know
I am walking on down
To the Tarwater tonight
See if I can't find to my delight
Someone who thinks artist
Are cute and fun
In the Tarwater tonight

Songs of the night train
At night the trains whistle
Is so clear
The sound on the tracks
Echo across the river
And come back up the hill
Sounds like the train is
Going to come down
My street
But alas it passes
And rolls down the Gorge
For someone else to
Write about the sound of the whistle
And the train rolling down the tracks

Tourist season in the Gorge
The weekend is so close
You can feel the excitement
In the air
On Thursday
A dribble of tourist
Slip into town
Into the stores
Out on the rivers
The trails
That night in the bars
Busier than normal
On Friday the dribble
Increases to a flow
Then late in the day
They swamp the area
Those without reservations
Driving around trying to find a room
Or campsite
The restaurants
Filling up as well
The bars overflowing
Out on the sidewalks
By Saturday morning
The rivers teaming with windsurfers
Kayakers' running the rapids
On the tributaries
The trails are hard to get to
As the parking is limited

Stores full of looky loos
Restaurants serving lunch and breakfast
Saturday night .... wild times
In the bars and the campgrounds
Sunday starts slow
Bacon cooking in the campgrounds
Breakfast in the restaurants
For those leaving early
Last minute windsurfers
Hikers taking short hikes
On the way out of town
In the afternoon 14 and 84
The highway to Goldendale
All busy
By late afternoon
Quiet in town
Traffic dying down
That evening in the bars
Locals and summer people
All gather and tell stories
Of the weekend onslaught
And on Monday morning
We are back to being
Just a small town
On a big river

Summer storms in the Gorge
The flash lights up the sky
The sound rolls across the countryside
The darkness moves across the land
The water pours down in sheets
The wind blows hot
Then cold as the mountain snows
Down the Gorge from east to west
It moves so steady across the horizon
You can watch its march
Up to your door best get inside
Before it starts to pour
Best not be seated in that aluminum chair
When the flashes are right above you

Ace hardware in White Salmon

Ace hardware in White Salmon
Has the best popcorn in all the land
Been to theaters all over the states
Never had popcorn as good as
Ace Hardware in White Salmon
Made my own spice and butter mix
For popcorn that I love
But truth is
Ace Hardware in White Salmon
Has the best popcorn in all the land
I can smell it when I drive past
I use ever excuse that I can
Or whatever reason I can think of
To go find something at
Ace Hardware in White Salmon
.

For the stars

The moon the moon
I'll dance to the moon
The moon the moon
I'll dance to the midnight light
I'll dance to the moon
While the stars watch on
The stars the stars
Are all out tonight
They will clap with delight as
I dance to the moon….
Tonight
On the river banks
Of the Columbia

I had to ask
The clouds are on the march
Moving across the sky
With such purpose
I must ask why
The clouds are in such a hurry
Moving so quickly
They seem almost blurry
I must ask why
To where do you rush off too
To where is it you must be
All in such a hurry
I must ask where
The clouds only speak to the
TV weather person
So I checked the daily weather
I must ask where
They are off to the north
For it tis the season they are most
Unexpected to arrive
I must ask why
Graduations all taking place
Weddings on the hour
And it is our time to shower

Day in a poet's life

The day was productive
Errands run
Meals done
Gardening was fun
Dogs all fed
The night is quiet
Time now for a little toke
See what kind of things are cooking
In my head
Poems and or songs
The beauty of the day
The frustrations that occurred
The satisfaction of gardens
Coming into shape
The meal like a chef had prepared it
The mountain was out today
The river white capped
With a slight breeze
The feel of that breeze
When it blows through
While you're working in the garden
All these things are fodder
For poems and songs
To fill another book

Little snow song
Snow snow snow
Just to let us know
We live in the Gorge
Just a little snow
To remind us
That this is still Gods land
And all in his hand
Snow snow snow

Small town on a big river

Small town on a big river
Life is just flowing on by
Either down the river
Or down the highway
Matters not to us
As we are just a
Small town on a big river
Anyone stops its only for a spell
They spend their money
Tell their tales of woe and wonder
Couple a days later they move on
Move on down the river
Small town on a big river
Only a few stays around
We make it sound like a chore
But don't tell anyone
How much we love living
Living in a
Small town on a big river

Singing in White Salmon

Some people sing
With a band behind them
Some people sing
With a big choir
When I sing
Out on my deck
There is a band of
Crickets
Just across the fence
They play right on que
And the rate is pretty cheap
For backup singers
I use some katydids
Chirping along in perfect time
Once in a while an owl joins in
Just few hoots in the right place
Some people have back up dancers
Dancing along
I have my little dogs
And we dance and sing
When the neighbors light goes on
We all get real quiet
I just hum along
Till the light goes out
Then we sing and dance
All night long
Good night White Salmon
Love you all

Made in the USA
Middletown, DE
07 September 2020